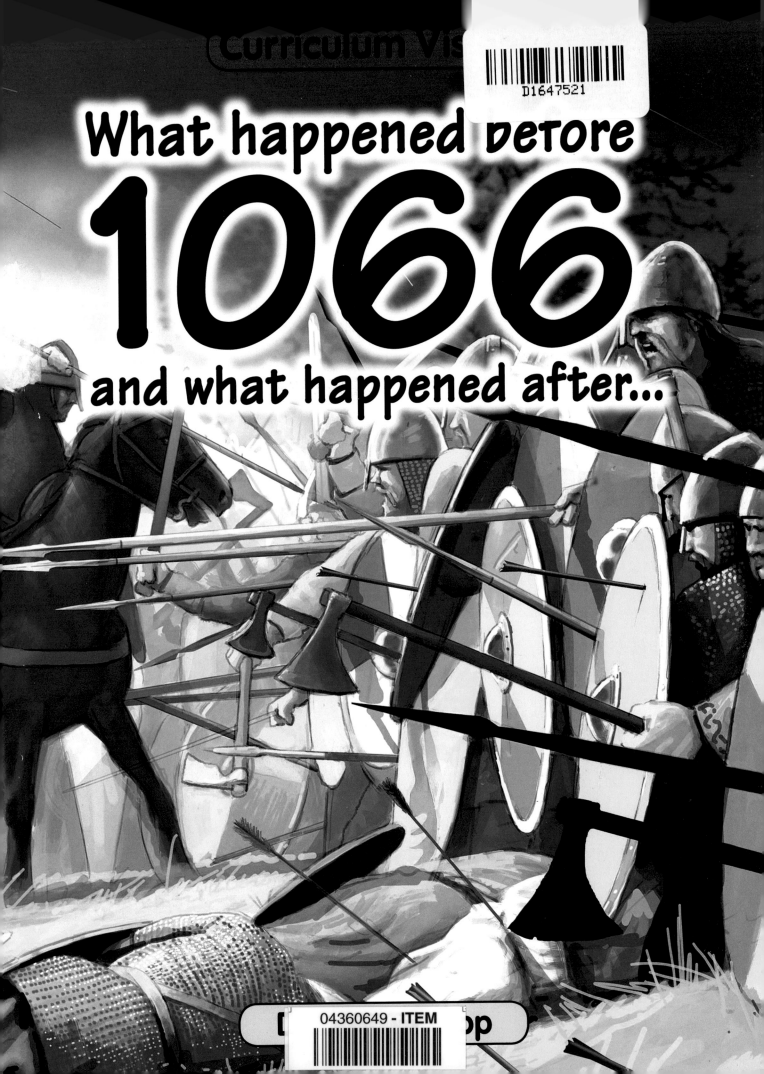

What happened before
1066
and what happened after...

World history

Ancient Egyptians (3000BC–332BC)

5000 BC	2000 BC	1000 BC

Sumerians (5000BC)

Maya (3000BC–1697)

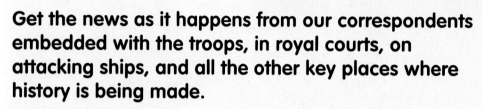

Get the news as it happens from our correspondents embedded with the troops, in royal courts, on attacking ships, and all the other key places where history is being made.

What would it be like if the Internet had existed in the past? We would have had news and opinions galore. Would it have changed the course of history? Who knows? But it is fascinating to see what it would have been like – and this is what we are going to do for the period before and after 1066.

We will assume that the reporters were all over the world beaming news into a central studio, just as they do today.

But, of course, these will be virtual reporters, and as there are very few eye-witness accounts of important events in the past, we will have to do our best to imagine what they might have said.

However, the facts, as best as we know them, will still be what you would find in any text book. But here you can enjoy finding out about a great event in history, and what happened afterwards, the modern way.

Saxon to Medieval timeline

Norman rule (1066-1154)

Saxon rule (approx 450-1066)

1066	1100	1200

Normans arrive

Tower of London

Battle of Hastings

William I 1066–1087 (The conqueror)
William II (Rufus) 1087–1100
Henry I 1100–1135
Stephen 1135–1154

Henry II 1154–1189 (archbishop Becket murdered)
Richard (the Lionheart) I 1189–1199 (Crusades)
(Bad) John 1199–1216 (Magna Carta 1215)
Henry III 1216–1272

Contents

Look up the words in **CAPITALS** in the glossary on page 46 of this book.

House of **PLANTAGENET** (1154–1485)   Houses of Lancaster and York (1399–1485)

1300   **1400**   **1485**

dward I (Longshanks) 1272–1307   The Wars of the Roses (14th and 15th centuries)   House of York (1461–1485)   Start of
   Edward II 1307–1327   House of Lancaster (1399–1471)   Edward IV 1461–1470   **TUDOR TIMES**
   Edward III 1327–1377   Henry IV 1399–1413   Edward IV 1471–1483
   Richard II 1377–1399   Henry V 1413–1422   Edward V 1483
     Henry VI 1422–1461 and 1470–1471   Richard III 1483–1485

The king is dead, long live who?

For nearly 700 years, the **ANGLO-SAXONS** (Saxons) had ruled all or most of England. But each king had to fight to keep control, for there were many people waiting to replace him. Some were Anglo-Saxon **NOBLES**, while others were rulers of other countries.

England was an attractive place to rule. It had minerals and crops that could be traded. And it gave the ruler power.

But who would rule was all very complicated. Since the 9th century **VIKINGS** had controlled parts of the country, and relatives of the Viking invaders still lived in Norway, Denmark – and **NORMANDY**.

If all went well, kings would pass on the crown to their sons. But if a king should die without an **HEIR**, then trouble was certain. Our story starts with King Edward (the Confessor), who was childless. He spoke French, he had lived in Normandy and was distantly related to the Vikings. But the Saxons, who were now in full control of England, wanted to have a Saxon king. By 1066 it was clear that Edward would soon die. So other people began making preparations...

From our English Court correspondent...

Rumour has is that Edward promised the throne to Harold **GODWINSON**. Harold is a Saxon and head of the most powerful family in the country, but he is not related to Edward, so this could lead to complications. We shall have to wait and see.

And now someone is coming out of the palace to speak to us. He is looking very grave. Here he is:

"I have to tell you that our King died a few minutes ago. The Witenagemot (Parliament) have met under the leadership of Lord Harold Godwinson, and they have unanimously elected Lord Godwinson to be our next king.

The king will be buried in the abbey today, and the coronation will take place immediately afterwards. God save the King. God save King Harold."

Note: Many pictures used have to be modern ones of what is left from the past, or what has replaced what existed in Norman times. Just keep this in mind.

Edward the Confessor ▶

EDWARD
the
CONFESSOR·

5

Long live the Viking king

As we have said, there were many people wanting the throne of England. One of those who felt he had a claim was the Norwegian king, but that was partly because he was having a difficult time at home, and he needed to divert attention away from domestic problems.

From our Norwegian Court correspondent...

Norway, August 1066

I am in Norway, in the court of King Harald Hardrada. Harald III has been King of Norway since Magnus I died in 1047. He is now 51 years old and has the nickname of 'Stern Ruler'. As it happens, Harald has not lived in Norway for much of his life. After a disagreement over the **SUCCESSION** to the throne, he was exiled and has spent much of his time in Constantinople (Turkey). He is reported to have been a brave warrior, and he made a fortune from his exploits, for, like all warriors, his reward for winning was a share of the **BOOTY** of those he had beaten.

It was a useful amount of money, because Harald was determined to go back to Norway and regain the throne, and for that he needed to pay for troops.

In 1046 Harald came back to Norway and was ready for a fight. But, I understand he agreed to share power with his ageing uncle Magnus. Shortly after this, Magnus 'died', and so Harald became King of Norway. Harald wanted the throne of Denmark, too, but he was not successful in this, and he has now given up any ideas of being King of Denmark – and that means he has lost face with his people.

So that is why he has turned his attention on England. In the early 1040s, England had been ruled by King Harthacnut, a Danish Viking. Harald claimed that Harthacnut and Magnus had agreed that, if either should die, the one who lived should rule over England, Denmark and Norway. And this is why, Harald tells me, when Harthacnut died, and Magnus became King of Denmark, he let Edward the Confessor become King of England. How complicated can it get?

But I am told by reliable sources, that there was no proof of this agreement, and even Harald would not have bothered about England if it had not been for Earl Tostig Godwinson, brother of King Harold Godwinson of England. Tostig was jealous of his brother. He is reported to have said to Harald "If you wish to gain possession of England, then I may bring it about that most of the chieftains in England will be on your side and support you".

That could be a deciding factor. So now we wait to see what is going to happen. Harald is not a young man any more, but he has always been greedy for more power...

▲ Harald Hardrada's monument in Oslo.

William – my rightful throne

Many years earlier, when Edward the Confessor (Duke William's cousin) was in **EXILE**, and before he was king of England, he promised the abbot of Fecamp Abbey in Normandy that it could own lands on the south coast of England, in gratitude for being allowed to stay in Normandy. Lands near Hastings had also been given by a former English king, Cnut.

This is partly what gave the Normans claim to lands in England, but the Saxons sent the monks packing back to Normandy in 1052 because they didn't want any Normans on their lands.

The Saxons who did this were led by the Godwinsons. But William of Normandy could use this to his advantage, claiming that he could get the abbey's rightful lands back. That also put him in favour with the Pope (although the Pope's price included more land if William won).

When it came to the time of the **INVASION**, the abbey even paid for one of the ships William used.

▶ We get only fleeting glimpses of what William looked like. Most of the statues were made hundreds of years after his death. Coins show his head. But none of these show what William looked like. They are PROPAGANDA pictures, designed to show William as a strong man.

From our Normandy court correspondent...

The news of Edward's death has reached the court here. The mood is bleak. Duke William is a fearsome ruler and he had expected to be called to be King of England because he was a cousin of childless Edward the Confessor. He is closest in blood line.

But the Godwinsons are the most powerful Saxon family in England, and they struggled with Edward the Confessor for power. It is a recipe for war.

William is now 38 years old, a towering 5ft 10inches tall and fighting fit. He can pull a bow more easily than most in his army, so is looked up to and respected.

But my sources also tell me that Duke William knows about another claim to the throne made by King Harald Hardrada of Norway. William fears he will have to deal with both Saxon Harold and Norwegian Harald if he is to be king of England. But whatever the odds, it is clear that William has decided to take England by force.

William's half-brother is Odo, Bishop of Bayeux. William is careful to keep on good terms with the church, as he needs their blessing if he is to go on campaigns and wars. For this purpose he has built twenty monasteries in Normandy alone. I hear that the Bishop of Bayeux has said he will make a tapestry of the events of the invasion after William wins the crown of England. Perhaps he should say 'if'...

The great Debate
I am now outside the court of William. He is gathered with his nobles as they plan the invasion of England. But there is much

concern. Are they strong enough to defeat Harold? Will their ships be sunk if a storm comes up while they are crossing the Channel? Will the Saxons simply kill them on the beaches as they try to land?

I hear that William has promised the other nobles a share of the lands and their wealth if they are successful in England. Of course that is what they expected. They have to pay for their own armies, after all. Nevertheless, everyone is cheered by this – they all understand about power and money.

William has also sent messengers to the Pope to get his blessing, and I understand that the Pope is happy with the invasion, provided the church is well rewarded. To prove the church is on their side he now has a Papal Banner to carry into battle.

Fecamp Abbey, Normandy.

The battles near Jorvik (York)

By the summer of 1066, Harold Godwinson knew he would have to fight for the throne he had held since December. He knew that he faced attack from the Vikings and also the Normans. But which would attack him first?

He didn't know, but he thought the Norman attack was the most likely, so he stationed his troops in the south of England, watched and waited.

But as it turned out, the Normans could not cross the English Channel because of rough seas. So, it was the Viking attack that happened first, and this meant that Harold had his main force far away from where the attack would come.

▼ **The Battle of Stamford Bridge.**

Our Viking correspondent reports on fact and heresay...

Fulford, 20th September 1066

I am here on the outskirts of the ancient city of Jorvik (also called York). I have been accompanying Harald Hardrada since his great fleet of Viking warships set out from Norway to attack England. The aim of this fleet is nothing short of taking control of the kingship and killing Harold Godwinson, king of England.

On this fleet of 300 **LONGSHIPS** we have counted about 11,000 warriors. We have spotted Earl Tostig, the brother of Harold, King of England. Some hereabouts have been calling him a traitor.

The fleet has come up the River Ouse towards the port of Jorvik, but an English army is already there, sent out from Jorvik. Its aim: to delay the Vikings until the main Saxon force can arrive – even if it means sacrificing every last man. The Saxons stand firm. The Viking army meets them on swampy land at a tiny village called Fulford just on the outskirts of Jorvik.

The English have about 6,000 men, just over half the number the Vikings brought with them. The Vikings easily outnumber the English. Even as battles go, this is turning out to be a bloody affair. The Vikings are hacking at the English with great ferocity, leaving a battlefield soaked in blood. The English have lost this battle – but gained time.

Stamford Bridge, 25th September 1066

Saxon King Harold has expected defeat at Fulford. But he cannot let the threat go unchallenged. Now we are off on a fantastic forced march, day and night, making 185 miles north in just 4 days. There is no way the Vikings will expect this. We are bound to catch them unawares.

I hear that the Viking army are scattered on both sides of the river Derwent, north of Jorvik, and are just relaxing. They appear to be without any armour.

Now the Vikings have spotted Harold's army coming over the rise in the land. I am watching as Hardrada's men try to hold the bridge and stop the English pouring over. One man valiantly stood on the bridge, for what seemed like ages, and I counted forty Saxons killed by him alone. But now one Saxon has stabbed at him from under the bridge and he has been felled.

Now the English are pouring over the bridge. The Vikings have set up a **SHIELD WALL**, but it is no use. The massacre is beginning. It is a bloodbath. Almost none of the Vikings will survive, and both Harald and Tostig have been hewn down. I watch more fighting until the Vikings begin to flee.

Only at the end is Harold prepared to offer a truce to the few Vikings who remain. There are only enough Vikings left to fill twenty four of their three hundred boats. The Vikings have promised Harold that they will never return. This has been a momentous day. What seemed like a Viking day of Victory has turned out to be, quite literally, the last day of the Viking Age in England.

▶ The memorial to the Battle of Stamford Bridge. So many died in an area so small that the field was said to have been still whitened with bleached bones 70 years after the battle.

The Normans are sighted!

Just after Saxon King Harold beat the Vikings, word reached him that the weather had turned favourable for the Norman invasion. There was simply no time to lose. Harold would have to move swiftly south again in order to stop William reaching London.

The best place to stop William would be in the hill lands of Kent, where routes were often reduced to narrow ridges, and it was easy to block the path of an army.

▶ The coast at Pevensey, looking west. You can see that the coast is a combination of high chalk cliffs and flat bays. The Normans would have to choose a bay. The beaches are all shingle, meaning that there was firm footing on the beach.

From our Home Affairs correspondent.

28th September 1066

I have had word that the **NORMANS** under Duke William have begun their invasion at last. Standing up here on Beachy Head, I can see almost to the other side of the English Channel. If there is to be an invasion, I will be one of the first to see it. But no one here is quite sure where the invasion fleet – if it comes – will land.

I have heard that advisors to King Harold are already on horseback, rushing to tell him about the invasion from Normandy. Of course, he is still up in Jorvik/York, having marched up to destroy the Vikings. So the Norman invasion will put him under great pressure, for his army will have to walk hundreds of miles south, having recently walked hundreds of miles north and fought a mighty battle. But Harold is a great leader, so if anyone is to make this incredible round trip, it will be him.

I am standing up here on top of these cliffs, but, of course, there is no way an army can land here, for the cliffs are too high. We know William will want to make straight for London, but will he land to the east, like the Romans did, or to the west, which is closer to Normandy? Near to us is Pevensey Bay, which is one possible site. And that is another reason I am here.

I have just been told – ships have been sighted on the horizon. Yes it is the Norman fleet. The invasion attempt is under way!

Pevensey is a perfect place for running a thousand ships aground, as the shingle beach makes firm ground for jumping ashore. I am not the first person to have stood on this spot. In fact, I am standing inside the remains of a fort the Romans built about eight hundred years before.

This may well be the site that William chooses to make as his base because, as any commander knows, you are very vulnerable when you land on a beach. You need to get off the beach and find a good place to defend. And what better than one already made by the Romans.

And yes, clearly the great fleet that we can see out in the Channel is making its way here. William must have had a lot of information about it. Of course we know why. Edward the Confessor had given lands near to here to one of the great Norman abbeys (Fecamp near Le Havre) and so many Normans have travelled here over the years. It would have been easy for William to get good knowledge of the whole area. And knowledge is power.

But landing and getting a strong foothold is one thing. An army must look for food. They are not going to get that in this marshland, so they must have a plan.

Walls of Roman fort

Norman castle

◀ Pevensey Castle, showing the outer Roman fort wall and the Norman castle built into a corner of it nearest the sea.

13

At Hastings

Pevensey was just a landing site and all around were marshes. William needed to find a place with a better route to London, so he moved his army on to Hastings. The site was a deep valley with high, defendable cliffs on either side. One of these was chosen as the site for a castle.

From our Correspondent embedded with the Norman invasion forces...

I am embedded with the troops of William. We are on horseback and moving with the **CAVALRY**, who are galloping quickly east. We think we know where they are going because there is a Saxon port ahead in an area of good farmland – and it is called Hastings.

We are watching while the troops help themselves to food. **PILLAGING**, as it is called, is not a pretty sight. Soldiers don't care about the people they take from, and if the people resist, they get mown down. We have just seen many cases of that on our journey to Hastings.

And now we have moved on to Hastings. The troops do not seem to want to move on any further, so we guess this must be the place where William wants to set up his base – his headquarters. He could not get his army assembled in the Pevensey marshes, but inland from Hastings the land is much easier. And we can see that assembling the army is going to take time because, although the

cavalry have arrived, the foot soldiers are nowhere in sight.

10th October 1066

I have been watching the troops play havoc in the Hastings area for nearly two weeks now. It is quite clear what the Normans have in mind: they want to make

Harold rush down from Yorkshire and fight them on their own chosen ground.

It's going to be a tough fight and I think William expects it to take a good few weeks before his rival can get down here.

So there seems to be no hurry.

▶ **Hastings Castle**

The battle nears

William had only 40 miles or so to reach London. Harold had nearly 200 miles to get down from York.

As the days went past, scouts were sent out to try to find out where the opposing army was.

It was now mid-autumn and the trees of the Kent forests were turning beautiful shades of yellow and brown. But looking at the forests was the last thing the leaders had on their minds. Each knew that in a few days one of them would be dead...

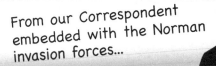
From our Correspondent embedded with the Norman invasion forces...

I am with William's troops, just north of Hastings.

Everything seems to be ready, and messengers have been arriving with news of the approaching English army, so there is great tension in the air.

Now the army is beginning to move inland along a long ridge that points directly towards London. They are bound to meet Harold somewhere along this route.

I have now come inland with the army of William and have reached the manor of Crowhurst. It is set in rolling countryside and is a very prosperous place.

I have just been told that this is the manor of Harold himself, and that the Normans are going to make a point of **SACKING** it just to make Harold even more angry. From where I stand I can see plumes of smoke rising from the burning buildings.

The army is now making surprisingly good progress. I had supposed it would be a slow trek, but in this area the Romans built roads to carry iron from their furnaces, and those roads still survive – and William is making good use of them.

Messages are now reaching us that Harold has made much faster progress than anyone had imagined. He is just a few miles ahead of us and he is barring our way, placing his army on high ground called Senlac Hill (Windmill Hill).

We have heard from the duke's men that William knows he must win battles before the winter sets in. Nobody fights battles in winter because the ground becomes too marshy, and food is much harder to find. So William is pressing on in order to secure the country before the winter comes. It makes winning all the more urgent.

I can see troops all around me, the question is whether William has sufficient troops or whether Harold's army will be bigger and more powerful. William has said that Harold has the advantage, for he can get men from anywhere. At the moment it is not clear who will win. The next few hours will be some of the most important the country has ever known.

From our Correspondent embedded with the Saxon forces on their way south...

I am embedded with Harold's troops. We have come down from Stamford Bridge. The king's strategy there was to take the fight to the enemy and surprise him. It looks as though Harold might be planning to do the same here.

This is hilly country, and ever since we have left London we have been travelling through wooded land. These forests stretch almost all the way to the south coast, and it will be impossible to fight a battle here. So what we expect Harold is doing is looking for a stretch of open farmland that he can use as a battlefield. And those are not very common along this road.

I am told that Harold is marching on without waiting to get his troops in better order because he thinks surprise is his best weapon. But the troops look very weary to me.

Now we have stopped on a hill with slopes leading up to us from the south. In the middle of it stands an apple tree. It is open ground here and an army can line up quite easily. We have stopped at a place where Harold thinks he has the advantage.

I am told that William is just a few miles away. He will have to approach us up the slope in front of me, but there is a marsh at the bottom. Alternatively, he can come along the ridge-top road, but Harold will easily be able to block that. In either case William's troops are at a disadvantage, so I am told that, although the Saxon troops are weary from their long march, they are full of confidence and ready to crush the Normans under the orders of their brave King Harold.

The Battle of Hastings, 1066

By October 14th, Harold and William were within a few miles of each other. We know approximately where they met because it is now marked by an abbey that William built after the battle. But as to the exact location of the battleground – that is uncertain. Many people think it is a slope facing south from the abbey, but no archaeological evidence has been found to tell of the battle – no shields, or weapons. But then they might all have been scavenged by people after the battle. So we can only guess what kind of ground the battle actually took place on. Here is one possible version.

From our Correspondent embedded with the Saxon forces...

14th October 1066

I am here on the hilltop with Harold's troops. We have taken up a defensive position on the hilltop, and the troops have all lined up with interlocking shields. Harold has just given the order to start beating the shields with swords, axes and other weapons.

Now the men are also shouting. The great chorus rings around the woods and fields. They are shouting "out, out, out" as they work themselves up into a frenzy before the battle starts.

The noise is deafening. It is designed to show strength – and frighten the enemy. I can't see any way that the Normans can break through this kind of wall. I can't even see any way that arrows can get through.

The troops here are almost all infantry – walking soldiers. They are

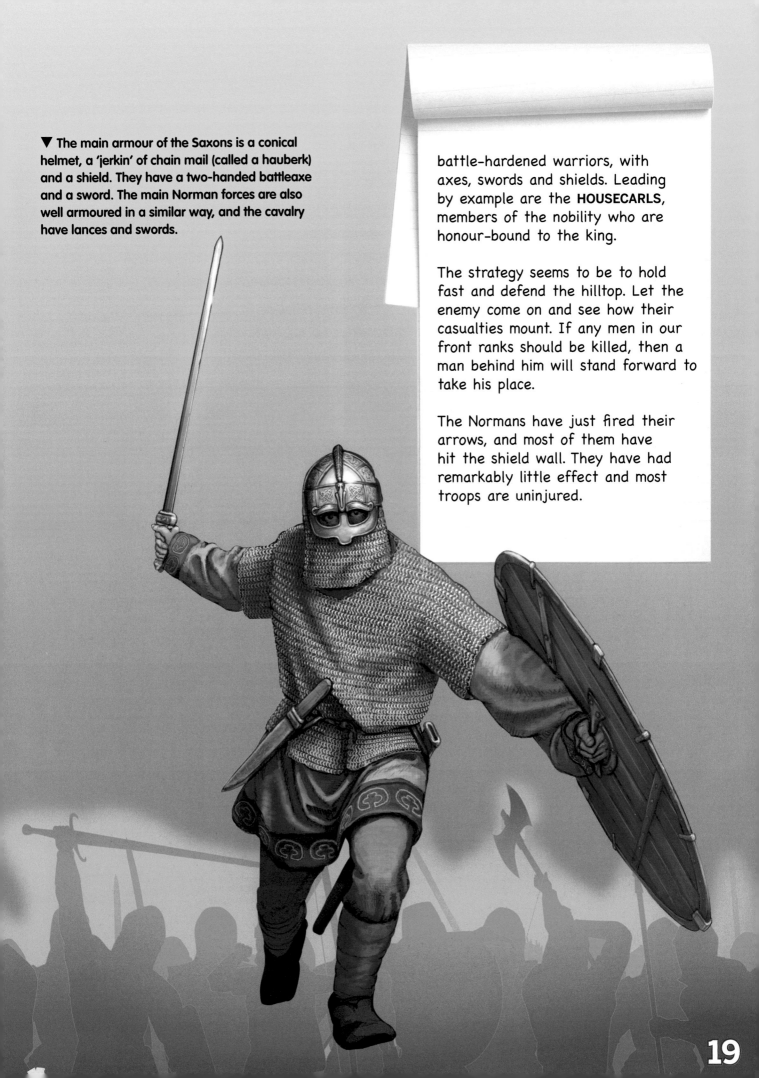

▼ The main armour of the Saxons is a conical helmet, a 'jerkin' of chain mail (called a hauberk) and a shield. They have a two-handed battleaxe and a sword. The main Norman forces are also well armoured in a similar way, and the cavalry have lances and swords.

battle-hardened warriors, with axes, swords and shields. Leading by example are the **HOUSECARLS**, members of the nobility who are honour-bound to the king.

The strategy seems to be to hold fast and defend the hilltop. Let the enemy come on and see how their casualties mount. If any men in our front ranks should be killed, then a man behind him will stand forward to take his place.

The Normans have just fired their arrows, and most of them have hit the shield wall. They have had remarkably little effect and most troops are uninjured.

I am here embedded with William's troops. On the far hill I can see Harold's troops, and now I can hear the dreadful din of the troops beating their weapons on their shields and shouting foul oaths at us.

We have lined up with archers in the front, infantry behind and cavalry on the side. This is an amazing sight. William has chosen to bring archers with **CROSSBOWS**, not the traditional **LONGBOW**. It is the first time in England that crossbows have been used. It is a big risk, and we shall soon see if it works.

The troops I am with have also now begun to beat their shields and shout. It cannot be long now before the battle starts.

William has many different kinds of troops, and I expect we will soon see him put his famous cavalry into action. But he must know that they will not be able to break through the Saxon shield wall.

The battle has begun, and William is getting his archers to send a barrage of arrows into the air.

The infantry is now ready to attack. William must think the archers have had some effect, but I cannot see any evidence of it. Here they go now, running up the hill to the shield wall.

▶ A pike. Pikes could not be used effectively in battle. They were mainly for defence.

I am standing behind Harold's troops. Now, as the Normans attack our position, the soldiers around me are throwing whatever they can find, not just lances, but also rocks and stones. It is working, the advance has faltered, and many Normans are felled.

Now I can see the Norman cavalry racing down the hill, into the valley and up towards us. But their horses do not like the shield wall and are turning away. Our forces seem to have the upper hand.

In front of me now are lines and lines of Norman bodies. We seem to be beating them back. And now I can see part of the Norman army fleeing.

Oh, no! Harold is not able to keep control of his army. They have sensed victory and are rushing down the hill after the fleeing Normans. The shield wall is pulling apart as more and more soldiers break ranks. Only the housecarls are standing firm. This can't be good for our Saxon side because the Norman cavalry can now attack more easily.

It is as I feared. The cavalry have been sent in again, and this time with great effect. Many of our troops are now slain, including both of Harold's brothers. Who now will rally the troops if Harold is killed?

We have now lost many of the housecarls, and the other kinds of soldiers are not as disciplined.

And here comes another hail of arrows from the Norman archers. It is killing many of the soldiers behind what is left of our shield wall.

I can no longer see Harold. Perhaps he has been killed. The men all around – except for the housecarls – are frightened and leaderless. Many are fleeing. I fear it will soon be over.

Our Norman war correspondent...

I can see our infantry moving up the hill, but the Saxons are now throwing lances and rocks at the infantry. They can't take much more of this. Things do not seem to be going the way that William wanted.

William is now sending in his cavalry. This seems a lot earlier than normal in a battle. Now the cavalry have charged, but the Saxon wall has stood firm.

They have been fighting for an hour now, and part of our forces are breaking and running away in disarray.

But now I see the Saxon shield wall breaking apart as the excited Saxons chase our troops down the slope. Surely this will give a chance for our cavalry to regroup and charge into them. Perhaps we have a chance after all.

William is now throwing rank after rank of men at the Saxons, and many of the finest Saxon warriors, the housecarls, have been slain.

Now William has used his archers again, firing over the remains of the shield wall into the Saxon men who are milling about leaderless behind it. Many have fallen, and it is reported that Harold is among them, though no one really knows.

This can't go on much longer. William is going to win after all.

William – the Conqueror

It was important for William and his small force to move quickly to London and seize control. One battle was not a victory – and William knew it. But he had one stroke of luck. So many of the Saxon nobles had been killed at Hastings that the Saxons were leaderless.

▼ Even four years after the battle, bones of some of the thousands who fell in battle still littered the site. Pope Alexander II ordered the Normans to do penance for killing so many people during their conquest of England. Some of the outbuildings of the abbey still remain, but nothing is left of the actual church. The battle may have taken place on the slope in front of where the abbey was built, but no one knows for sure.

▼ This plaque marks the spot of the High Altar in Battle Abbey. Most of the abbey was destroyed by Tudor King Henry VIII in 1538 at a time called the Dissolution of the Monasteries. All that is left of the abbey church itself today is its outline on the ground.

From our correspondent accompanying the victorious, and rather nervous, Normans...

It is the day after the great battle north of Hastings. I am still embedded with the Normans. After the bloodshed and effort of the battle yesterday, the troops are resting. Many are very ill, suffering from exhaustion and stomach bugs. Even William is ill. But we hear that reinforcements are coming from Normandy. Still, there is no dispute about who is to be king of England.

As I stand with King William close to the battlefield, I have to report to you several momentous things that have happened in the space of a few weeks. Harold ended the age of the Vikings a few short days ago and now William has ended the age of the Saxons. So, in a few short days, the whole way that England has been governed for five hundred years has been overturned.

As I look around the battlefield today, I see many of the Saxon lords lying slain. There will be no lord of the manor in many places, and far fewer to help govern the country. But even so, the great majority of the people of this fair country did not take part in any of the battles. It was a war between nobles and a few thousand soldiers, that is all. It will be a country of Saxons (and Vikings) ruled by a few Normans. The Normans will not be able to do it on their own. They will need help. For one thing, they cannot speak the language of the Saxons.

I have just heard news that King William will go to Westminster in London to be officially crowned. It will be interesting to see, though, what the Pope makes of all the bloodshed in the lands the Norman army has marched through, for many would say it was not necessary to kill so many civilians as well as the troops of Harold's army.

It is Christmas Day 1066. I am reporting from outside Westminster Abbey where Edward the Confessor was laid to rest so recently.

The journey from Hastings has not been without its troubles. The Saxons tried to crown a new king, Edgar, but there was no strong leader left. No one is even sure if he was crowned or not.

The people of London have resisted the advance of William's troops, and so he has had to go round the city, cross the Thames at Wallingford, and attack from the north.

The Londoners have seen that further resistance is useless, and have surrendered.

This is the final moment of the invasion. The course of history has been changed in England. But I wonder what will happen next? After all, the small number of Normans are still in a largely hostile land. William will have to put into action a plan, and I hear that he is already building a castle in London, a single tower of wood. We suspect that, as soon as possible, he will replace that with a permanent one using some stone from his home of Normandy. If so, this White Tower of limestone will become the Tower of London and England's most important castle. The king's capital, presently at Winchester, will soon be moved to London.

▼ Westminster Abbey where William was crowned.

▼ The keep at the Tower of London begun by William the Conqueror.

25

The Bayeux Tapestry

From our home affairs correspondent.

Bayeux, Normandy, France, 1077

I have come to look at one of the most remarkable pieces of art ever made. It is a story of the events that led to the crowning of King William I – and it has been stitched by ladies!

The idea was put about by the half-brother of King William, Bishop Odo, to make a piece of art for his victorious relative, and to put it on display for evermore in the cathedral which has been under construction at Bayeux in Normandy.

Bishop Odo's idea was to hang this great length of embroidered cloth on the wall of the cathedral. Because it is a cloth for hanging, it is called a tapestry.

But it was not made by Norman women. Instead it was embroidered by the very people that William conquered, that is the Saxon ladies of Kent, where Odo had been given estates. So why did he do it in Kent? The answer is that the most skilled needlework throughout Europe was done in Kent. This part of England was famous for it. The ladies of Bayeux had absolutely nothing to do with it because they were simply nowhere near as skilled as the English ladies of Kent.

There is no doubt that it is a great work of art. But is it accurate history, my fellow correspondents have been

asking? They think it is a piece of propaganda, designed to show William at his best, and to show how he had a right to the crown of England.

For example, it shows all of Harold's men fleeing from the battlefield after he was killed, but our correspondent embedded with the Saxons says that they mostly fought bravely to the death.

As you would expect, the main character of the tapestry is William.

The tapestry begins with King Edward the Confessor, who has no son and heir. Edward sends Harold Godwinson to Normandy to tell William that he had decided that William should become king on his death. While in Normandy, Harold fights on the side of William in several battles. While he is there, William makes Harold take an oath to allow William to take the throne. Harold then goes back to England, but on Edward's death, Harold takes the crown.

This makes William enraged and he plans to invade England to claim the crown promised him by Edward.

It all takes time to build a fleet of ships, get an army together and more. But, by summer 1066 he is ready. He lands on the coast and the army have a great feast before doing battle with the Saxons.

During the battle Harold is often close to winning, but, according to the tapestry, he is killed with an arrow in his eye. William claims the throne and becomes the King of England.

But it is not that clear, my fellow correspondents have been saying. No one is sure about the fate of Harold. The part of the tapestry showing an arrow in the eye is not proof, because it is common to show people who have broken an oath with an arrow in the eye, and the Normans believed Harold broke his oath to William. Our correspondent embedded with the Saxons did not see the killing, so there are no witnesses to what really happened.

After 1066: King, Domesday and Parliament

After the conquest was settled, William was rarely in England. It was his nobles who ran the country. But although William had given most of the land to nobles and church, he was owed taxes from much of it, and he was not sure he was getting what he was due. This is why he commanded a book of taxes to be made. It was the Domesday Book.

Of course, the arrival of the **NORMANS** brought great change, and this is why the time starting from the Battle of Hastings is called the Middle Ages, or Medieval times.

Normans and PLANTAGENETS

Medieval times lasted for 400 years. They were marked by more or less continuous war between kings and nobles, England, Scotland, Wales and France. And it was all the result of a Norman (French) duke becoming king of England.

The first of the kings after 1066 was Norman William I. Among the long line of kings that followed through the Middle Ages, there were some extraordinary people, such as Richard I (the Lionheart), King John (of Robin Hood and Magna Carta fame) and Edward I (who built great castles all around Wales).

The Normans spoke French because they came from France. Even Richard the Lionheart – popularly thought of as a very English king – only spoke French.

The early kings lived at the time of the Crusades, and Richard I was a crusader. He spent most of his time away from England, and the country was ruled by his brother, John.

◀ Richard I (Richard the Lionheart) has a statue in front of the Houses of Parliament. He was hardly ever in England and did not even leave an heir.

▲ Part of the Domesday Book.

When Richard died, John became king in his own right. John is famous for trying to keep power to himself, much to the displeasure of the nobles. As a result, they banded together and forced the king to sign an agreement setting out what the king's powers were – and more importantly to them – what rights the nobles had. This is called the Magna Carta.

One of the most important medieval kings was Edward I. He was a very strong king. He spent much of his time in wars with the Welsh and the Scots, as they fought to decide who would control the land. It was because of this that Edward had castles built all around Wales. But he did far more than that, including setting out our legal system and making the foundations of **PARLIAMENT**.

From our financial affairs correspondent...

The king has been on the throne for nearly 20 years now and he is getting increasingly more confident that he has the country under control. Many new castles have been built and land distributed among his barons. The king is a very wily man. He has given lots of land to the church (as he promised them for calling the invasion 'the will of God') and he had given his barons much, but only on condition that they protect what they have been given, and guarantee to supply troops in times of needs. So, in fact, the burden of keeping an army going has been taken away from the king and put on the shoulders of his barons. The king has kept about a quarter of all land for himself.

But over the years, the king has become increasingly worried that he may not be getting as much money by way of taxes as he should. So this Christmastime, while he was staying in Gloucester, he was deep in conversation with his officials. I can now report what they decided. They are going to send men to every part of England and "make a record of what or how much each landholder has in land and livestock, and what it is worth".

The whole result will be collected and made into two huge reference books and used to make decisions on taxes.

There will be no right of appeal. And it is all to be kept in a special chest in the royal treasury at the Norman capital city of Winchester. As a result, the books are called the Book of Winchester, but they are sure to become known by their nickname, the Domesday Books, meaning the Day of Judgement. So now it seems there are only two things you cannot avoid in Norman England: death and the tax man. I wonder if that will change in a thousand years time?

▲ Magna Carta

1215 Runnymede, Berkshire

I am standing here on the banks of the River Thames near Windsor witnessing a most extraordinary sight. In front of me there are tents belonging to many famous barons of this land and also to our king, John I.

They are about to sign a treaty that will be one of the most famous the world will ever see. It is to be called Magna Carta.

This signing has been long in the making. In 1066, William the Conqueror introduced a **FEUDAL SYSTEM**. He gave out lands to his barons (who were called his tenants-in-chief) and church leaders. This feudal system required the king to seek the advice of the barons and the church before making new laws. But King John wanted none of it and so the barons have threatened to rebel – and they have more force on their side than the king. So now the king is being forced to sign a document saying that the king may not levy or collect any new taxes until he has the consent of the barons who will be called the Royal Council. (this will later be called **PARLIAMENT**).

▲ Edward I – known as 'longshanks' because he was so tall – was one of the greatest fighting kings in English history.

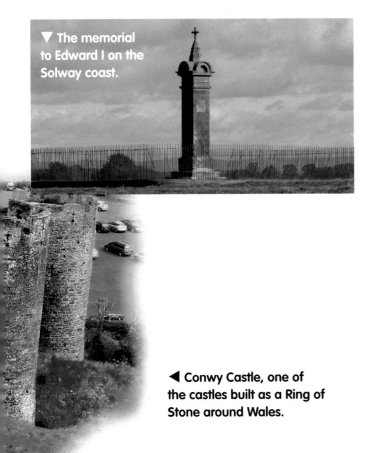

▼ The memorial to Edward I on the Solway coast.

◄ Conwy Castle, one of the castles built as a Ring of Stone around Wales.

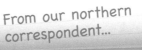
I am standing here on the flat marshes of the Solway Firth, looking across the grey waters towards Scotland.

I am just outside the tent of our king, Edward I. Edward has been preparing for battle against the Scots again, and this time he is determined to take control. He has already subdued the Welsh and built a ring of castles around Wales which we call the **RING OF STONE**. He thought he had subdued the Scots, too, when he executed rebellion leader William Wallace, and this is how he got the name "Hammer of the Scots". But now another leader has emerged – Robert the Bruce, who has just murdered his rival and had himself crowned King of Scotland. Edward now intends to rid Scotland of treacherous Robert.

Or at least he did. But a few days ago the king was taken ill with dysentery. He got worse and worse, and I have just been told that he has passed away peacefully inside his tent.

This is no time to continue the battle. It is time to remember what he left for England. We remember, in particular, that he set out a legal code for the country for the first time. It is a code which we expect will last a thousand years. He has also set up Parliament in a right and proper fashion to try to unite England, Scotland and Wales. Edward declared that everyone in the Kingdom who thought they had been badly treated could submit petitions to Parliament. Parliament would then resolve them and so stop nobles and others going to war with one another. (Submitting a petition to Parliament is a tradition that continues to this day.)

Let us hope that the good works done by Edward will not be wasted.

Village life in feudal times

How did life change for the majority of people during the Middle Ages? At first, things changed very quickly, as Normans built castles to protect themselves in case the Saxons rose up against them. They also brought the **FEUDAL SYSTEM**, and many ordinary people found themselves not much better off than slaves. But they got used to it.

Over time, most people in the countryside settled down to the feudal way of living run by lords in the castles and the abbots in their monasteries.

From our rural affairs correspondent...

I have just been walking around the village. Nothing much has really changed in the centuries since castles and monasteries were built at the start of Norman times. Everyone still lives in the village, supposedly protected by the lord. They work in the great fields owned by the lord and the church, and they mostly live in small hovels.

There are a few 'free' men who have been granted special rights and own their own land. They are called yeomen, and they live in bigger houses. Because they can keep all the money made on their land, they do not have to pay a tenth to the lord or church.

Because the roads are very poor, most people prefer to travel by boat to nearby towns and villages.

Many buildings combine a house with a barn. There are no chimneys.

Large fields surround the village. They are divided into strips, and each farmer has a number of strips in different fields. One field is always left unploughed, or fallow, to give the soil a chance to recover after producing a crop. Beyond the fields is forest.

The mill is important because it is where people grind their grain.

The church is the largest building. It might still have an Anglo-Saxon tower. Most likely, it would have been rebuilt and all traces of the Anglo-Saxon church would have been destroyed.

The 'hall house' – the biggest house in the village – is home to a rich YEOMAN.

The paths in the village are muddy and covered in animal and human waste.

From time to time, markets are held in an open space in the village.

Many homes are long and thin and used for people and animals. They have a small patch of land behind, for growing vegetables and keeping pigs and chickens.

Nearby is a castle, where the wealthy lord lives.

Feudal homes and living

From Norman to Tudor times, nothing much changed in the village because it worked under the feudal system. Most of the houses and land were owned by the Lord of the Manor or the Abbot. These powerful people take rents from the **PEASANTS** who live in their houses, and they also get a tenth part (called a **TITHE**) of everything the peasants grow.

Villages did have a few better-off people. They were called yeomen. But no matter what their size, most houses in our village consisted of a single room.

Each home (other than a castle or monastery) was made using a frame of timber posts cut from the nearby forest. The walls were made with straw, dung, mud and twigs. It was called wattle and daub. Others were made with strips of wood, called laths, covered with plaster. Inside every home the floor was earth. There were few built fireplaces or chimneys. The fire was simply made on the floor in the centre of the room. Its smoke made the whole house black with soot. There was no ceiling. You looked straight up to the roof.

▼ Nobleman's hall house.

▼ Peasant's house

I am reporting to you as I row away from a small village I have just been visiting. What was it like? Well, it stinks. Of course, that is nothing new because all the waste is in the streets. And people don't bother to go out of their homes to do their business. They just do it on the floors of their homes.

Most people live in small hovels, one room for sleeping and eating, which they share with their animals. They have trestle tables, and at night they take the table boards off, put them on the floor and sleep on them.

While I was there, they were punishing someone in the pillories. They were throwing rotten food at him – and worse. Still, being in the pillories is much better than some of the punishments the villagers get - like chopping off an ear – something called 'cropping'. Unless, that is, the villagers decide to throw bricks and stones – and then the poor fellow might get killed.

I hoped I would get to visit the lord, for at least in their castle they have sweet smelling herbs and rushes strewn over their floors. But my luck was out, so I am really glad to be back out on the river.

▼ Pillories

Town life

While little changed in the countryside, some towns became wealthier. Much of this wealth came from wool.

Wool was brought from the countryside and sold in the towns and cities – mostly through great yearly fairs. Traders (**MERCHANTS**) came from all over Europe to buy English wool at these fairs.

Wool was taken to Europe, where it was made into cloth. But then English merchants started to make cloth for themselves, and in this way they kept more of the profits. As a result, wool towns became among the most wealthy places in the country, with grand churches.

From our rural affairs correspondent...

I have now travelled by boat up the river to the nearby town. It is near to an abbey. The abbey is the wealthiest place and needs many goods and services. This helps to support the craftsmen and merchants in the town.

The town's main street runs from the ford to the abbey. Merchants and other wealthy people have built their houses close to the abbey, leaving the smelly trades like tanning, and dangerous trades like brickmaking, to spread out on the more floodable land by the river.

From what I can see, the town is getting wealthier, with people making goods in every doorway. But most of the money comes from people tucked away in their houses making cloth for the merchants.

Mill

▼ **The street plans of Tudor towns still survive today in some places.**

Abbey

Merchant's house

Marketplace

Inn

Basketmaker's

Brewer's

Brickmaker's

Potter's

Tannery

37

The growing power of cities

Towns were getting wealthier, but the real power lay in the cities. Cities had been protected behind walls since Roman times. They worked very well because there was no national police or army. In Medieval times city people had reason to become even more anxious, as nobles and king fought one another, and the walls were strengthened.

Trade was growing in England, despite all the upheavals of fights between kings and nobles. Wool was the main reason for city growth, just as in some towns. Some cities even minted money.

The cities were run by wealthy merchants, who formed themselves into guilds to protect their interests.

Cathedral or Abbey

Bridge

Guildhall

River

Chain across river, usually left on the river bed and raised in times of attack.

Farmland

Trading wharves

Moat

Wall

In early Medieval times, these cities looked almost like countryside enclosed by walls. There were orchards and large areas for growing vegetables and keeping animals. But as more people moved to them, so the farmland inside the walls was gradually taken over for housing, and houses were built closer and closer together, so that many streets became little more than narrow alleys.

From our home affairs correspondent...

I have just been to the walls of the city. The king is visiting, but he must ask permission to enter. It is just a formality, but the city jealously guards the rights given to it in their charter. They were given the right to raise walls, and control who goes in and out. And they do.

Towns have steadily become more prosperous, and they are home to wealthy merchants and craftsmen. All of these people have formed into groups, called guilds, and now they run more or less everything in the city.

I have just had a meeting with the head of one of the guilds in their meeting room, or guildhall, to ask them why there are city walls and guilds. I was told that these were still unstable times, as nobles and their armies were likely to fight it out among themselves, and cities often wanted no part in it. So the walls were to keep everyone out. As for the guilds, well they stop other people from making the same goods, keep prices up, and make sure the wealth stays in the hands of a select group of craftsmen who can then maintain high standards. It is the feudal system at work.

Castle

39

Alone in the countryside

Although many areas of England were densely settled, there were still huge areas where there were very few people, which were out of reach of the big castles, and as a result where there was simply no law and order.

The most vulnerable area was in the north of England, along the border with Scotland.

There was constant risk of war with Scotland, and Scottish armies were sure to see what pickings they could get on their way south.

But it was not just an occasional war that farmers had to worry about. There was a much more clear and present danger than that. Border raiders – horse and cattle thieves called **REIVERS** – lived in this area. It meant that farmers had to live in fortified houses that were almost like mini-castles.

It was like living in a kind of 'Wild West', where you had to know how to look after yourself, and where you kept your animals inside as much as you could.

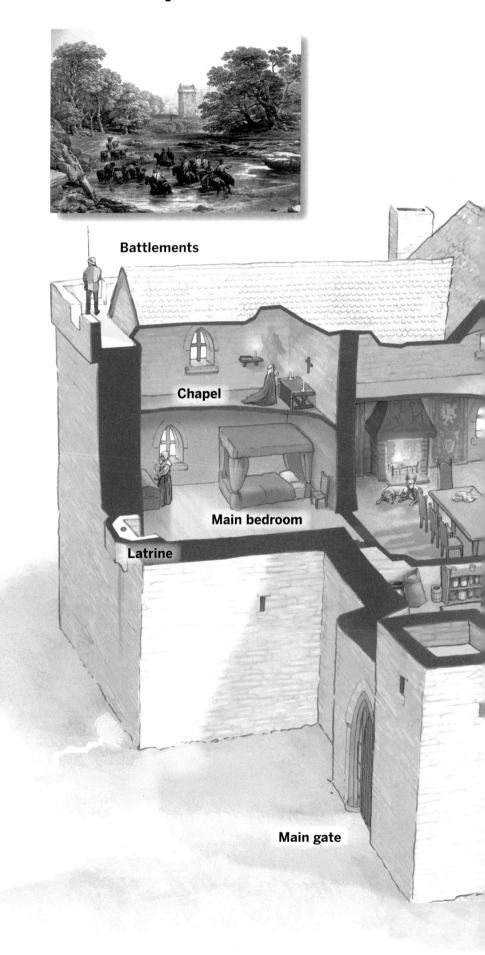

Battlements

Chapel

Main bedroom

Latrine

Main gate

It is not good news. I was staying with a family in their fortified house when news came that the reivers had been past and stolen many of the cattle over night.

They could not move quickly with the cattle so there was a real chance of catching them. So some men on horseback were despatched to catch them before they got to Scotland.

But, as it turned out, the reivers had no intention of running off with the cattle. Instead, they lay in wait for our men, and slaughtered every last one in an ambush. Then they rode off with what they really wanted – the horses.

reat
all

No low-level windows

Dungeon

◀ Fortified houses were so well defended, they were rarely attacked by force. Sometimes they were put under siege.

The Wars of the Roses

Of all the many wars of Medieval times, the most important was called the Wars of the Roses. It was a civil war, it brought Medieval times to an end, and started the time of the Tudors. This is how it happened.

The royal line splits

The Wars of the Roses was a power struggle between two branches of the royal line. It happened because, at this time, the king was often not very powerful, all nobles had their own armies and they fought for power using their own men.

Quite extraordinarily, during early Medieval times – from 1189 to 1399 – the crown was passed down the same family line. However in 1399 the then King Richard II decided to remove his cousin, Henry, from any claim on the throne. He forced Henry into exile. This caused great upset among the English nobles.

Richard II was not popular. This meant that, when exiled Henry decided to return and invaded England in June 1399, his army quickly grew in numbers. Henry defeated Richard and had himself crowned as King Henry IV.

Henry had broken the royal line by taking the kingdom by force. Powerful nobles realised that from now on, anyone with any kind of royal connection could seize power.

Henry's mother was Blanche of Lancaster and this is why Henry became the first King of England from the Lancaster branch of the royal line.

Lancaster Rose

The other powerful royal branch was those who belonged to the House of York. From now on it was going to be a difficult situation.

Eventually one of the Lancastrian kings was murdered, and the direct Lancastrian line to the throne was ended. That left the way open for Edward (from the York branch of the family) to be crowned as Edward IV.

The end of the wars

Edward IV died unexpectedly in 1483. His son, Edward, just 12 years old, was next in line for the throne. Edward IV's brother, Richard, was named as Protector of England. Richard took Edward and his brother to

▼ When you look at Tudor symbols you will see a rose everywhere. It is a double rose, made up of petals from both the Red Rose of the House of Lancaster, and the White Rose of the House of York. So the Tudor rose you see is no mere decoration. It is a symbol that the Wars of the Roses were over and that the two parts of the royal line were united again.

York Rose

Tudor Rose

the Tower of London, and they were never seen again. Meanwhile, Richard succeeded in getting the prince's claim rejected by Parliament, and that is why it was Richard who was crowned King Richard III on 6 July 1483.

Richard was king for two years when the final part of the Medieval drama unfolded. This was because Richard's claim to the throne did not go unchallenged.

Henry Tudor was a Lancastrian, and had been exiled for most of his life. Now he was able to raise an army in France and sail to Wales where he got further support. The final

battles of the Wars of the Roses were about to come to a head.

The final battle was fought at Bosworth Field, near Loughborough in the English Midlands. At this battle (described on the next page) Richard III was killed, and Henry Tudor was victorious. Henry Tudor had pledged to marry Elizabeth of York if he won. By doing this he brought the two royal lines together again, and from that point on **TUDOR TIMES** began.

The Battle of Bosworth Field

I am on a hill looking out over the battle that will take place at Bosworth Field. I am with Lord Stanley and his troops. I have Richard III and his troops on my right, and Henry Tudor and his troops on my left. Lord Stanley is not taking sides yet, so his men stand fast. I expect he is waiting to see who is going to win. He will then join the winning side.

Richard is dividing his army into three groups. On the right are a group with pikemen protecting 1,200 archers and some cannon. In the centre I can see Richard himself, at the head of some cavalry and 3,000 infantry. On the left is a group of 4,000 more men, most of them cavalry.

Henry's commanders, with fewer men, have all been kept together in one group. Henry is relying on a core of nearly 2,000 French mercenaries, helped by 1,000 English and 2,000 Welsh.

The battle has started. A great roar is reverberating across the countryside, as each leader encourages his troops to whoop and shout. They must be ready for battle. Now archers on both sides let go a hail of arrows.

Richard is the first to make a move. He has sent one of his groups into the attack while his cannon open fire over their heads. As neither side had been beaten back by this attack, they are now resorting to hand to hand fighting among infantry.

But just a minute. Something strange is happening. Some of Richard's troops have fled the battlefield because they don't see an easy victory. This is a bad sign.

There is worse to come. The second of Richard's groups will not move forward even though Richard has signalled them to do so. Richard must be worried. He has sent a message up here to tell Lord Stanley that he has one of his sons a prisoner and will have his son killed if he does not join him. It has not worked. Stanley has just sent a message back. It reads: "I have other sons."

Now it is clear that the battle will go Henry's way unless Richard does something really dramatic.

But now Henry Tudor is riding up here to meet the Stanleys. This must leave Henry open to attack.

Oh, my gosh! Richard clearly feels he has no choice but to risk everything

by making a charge to reach Henry and kill him. If Henry's troops are leaderless, they will turn and run. Richard has a huge force of cavalry with him – I suspect it is close on a thousand men.

The king is mounted on a white horse, and with his loyal cavalry they have begun their charge. But it is now quite obvious to the Stanleys which side they should be on, so they are rushing to help Henry. Right across the battlefield I can hear Richard yelling out 'Traitor!'

I think Richard's gamble might work. Richard is a brave soldier and he leads the charge. He has got as far as Henry's standard bearer and killed him. But his horse has now got stuck in the mud of the marsh and Richard is forced to the ground, losing his helmet in the process. His followers are all offering their own horses, but Richard, presumably seeing all is lost, has refused, and fights on foot. I can't bear to watch.

Now Richard is surrounded by Henry's troops. He is being beaten to the ground. He has been killed by a blow of a halberd from one of Henry's Welsh infantry. It is all over. Someone rushes to Richard to pick the crown out of the mud and gives it to Henry.

Long live the king.

Glossary

ANGLO-SAXONS The Anglo-Saxons were people who invaded from what is now Northern Germany, Holland and part of Denmark during the 5th and 6th centuries. They took advantage of the departure of the Romans which left England undefended. They set up new settlements and took over settlements of the British (Celts). The Anglo-Saxons named their villages, which is why we have more knowledge of them than the Celts.

BOOTY Any treasure gained by taking it from someone else by force.

CAVALRY Mounted soldiers. There have always been two kinds of cavalry – light cavalry who rode with less armour and smaller horses and who were very fast, and heavy cavalry, whose riders tended to be nobles and who were heavily armoured and rode carthorses. The heavy cavalry were the medieval form of tanks, and were very hard to stop.

CROSSBOW A bow fired with the bow lying flat. Crossbows fire short arrows known as bolts.

EXILE To be sent away from the home country and forced to live abroad. This was a punishment instead of execution, but it often backfired because it meant the exiled person could always raise an army abroad and then return.

FEUDAL SYSTEM The system introduced to England by the Normans in which there were the nobles, whose duty was to protect, the church, whose duty was to pray, and the peasants, whose duty was to work. The feudal system involved peasants giving a share (a tenth, or tithe, of what they produced, or a tenth of their labouring time, to work on the land of their lord).

GODWINSON, HOUSE OF The most powerful of the Saxon nobility was the House of Godwinson. Harold II was the leader of this noble house and the last Saxon king of England.

HEIR Someone who is named to succeed you. In Medieval times it would be a son, but it could be someone that had been named and was not a relative.

HOUSECARL The name for the nobles in Saxon times.

INVASION An attack on another country.

LONGBOW A bow held so that the bow is vertical. A longbow is a much longer bow than a crossbow and fires an arrow. The bow has a much longer reach than a crossbow.

LONGSHIP A form of galley which is propelled by oars when near to land, and a square sail when away from the coast. All peoples in ancient times, from the Greeks onwards, used longboats, although they are most popularly associated with Vikings.

MERCHANT A merchant was a kind of wholesaler, a businessman who bought in goods from farmers, miners and so on, and then sold them on to other people to be made into finished goods. Merchants did not sell to the public directly and so were not shopkeepers. You needed to be quite wealthy to be a merchant.

NOBLE People who were wealthy and had large amounts of land. They would be expected to help the king to rule the country, and swear an oath to fight with him when necessary in exchange for their land.

NORMANDY The north-western part of what is now France.

NORMANS The people who lived in Normandy. The noble who ruled Normandy was a duke, who owed allegiance to the King of France, but was effectively an independent ruler. William I was Duke of Normandy, and he regarded the Dukeship of Normandy as being more important than the Kingship of England.

PARLIAMENT An assembly of representatives who meet together to try to make laws that govern a country.

PEASANT A peasant is a farmer who lives from a small plot of ground, often divided up into long strips and part of his lord's great fields.

PILLAGING To take food and anything else of value from an area. Medieval armies lived off the land they conquered, so pillaging was commonplace.

PLANTAGENETS The line of rulers who followed the Normans as kings of England. The Normans and Plantagenets were related, and the word Plantagenet was a nickname given to the rulers many years afterwards. They did not call themselves Plantagenets.

PROPAGANDA Interpreting a set of acts in such a way as to give a distorted impression of those facts. That is, giving just one favourable side of a story.

REIVERS The word reiver comes from any ancient word meaning 'to rob'. They lived in the wild and lawless border regions of southern Scotland and northern England, where it was hard to make a living by farming, and easier to make a living by robbing. Reivers were families who owed no allegiance to any king.

RING OF STONE The Ring of Stone castles built by King Edward I to keep down the Welsh, and prevent them from rebelling. They were built after the Welsh uprisings when the Welsh princes refused to recognise the authority of Edward of England. It was the largest building project anywhere in Europe during the whole of the Middle Ages. The castles include Conwy, Harlech, Caernarfon and Beaumaris.

SACKING To destroy a place that has been captured by taking away all of its valuables, burning it, and reducing the buildings to rubble.

SHIELD WALL A defence that foot soldiers (infantry) used. It had been used since Roman times. The infantrymen overlapped shields, 'locking' them together so there was no way the attackers could get through. Pikes were jabbed over the shield wall at the attackers.

SUCCESSION A line of people who follow in from one another.

TITHE A kind of tax payable by the peasant to his lord (nobleman or abbot). It was about ten per cent of what a peasant produced each year.

TUDOR TIMES The period of just over one hundred years and which was begun by Henry VII in 1485. The Tudors mark the end of the Wars of the Roses. The Tudor monarchs were among the most famous England has ever had, and included Henry VIII and Elizabeth I.

VIKING Someone whose homeland is in the Scandinavian countries of Denmark, Norway and Sweden. The majority of Vikings who came to live in England were Danish.

YEOMAN The name probably comes from an old term meaning 'young man'. Yeomen were nearly nobility, but not quite. They may have been given land for some duty or task they did for the lord or king. As a result they did not rent it from a lord and this made them quite wealthy. They often held important positions in the parish where they lived, such as constable or bailiff.

Index

Curriculum Visions

There's more online
See our great collection of page-turning books and multimedia resources at:

www.CurriculumVisions.com

(Subscription required)

© Atlantic Europe Publishing 2014

The right of Brian Knapp to be identified as the author of this work has been asserted by him in accordance with the Copyright, Designs and Patents Act 1988.

Author
Brian Knapp, BSc, PhD

Senior Designer
Adele Humphries, BA, PGCE

Editors
Gillian Gatehouse
Emily Pulsford, BA

Illustrations
Mark Stacey

Designed and produced by
Atlantic Europe Publishing

Printed in China by
WKT Company Ltd

What happened before 1066 and what happened after... – Curriculum Visions
A CIP record for this book is available from the British Library.

Paperback ISBN 978 1 78278 079 3

Picture credits
All photographs are from the Earthscape and ShutterStock Picture Libraries.

This product is manufactured from sustainable managed forests. For every tree cut down at least one more is planted.